# Colors

# Red

## by Sarah L. Schuette

Reading Consultant:
Elena Bodrova, Ph.D., Senior Consultant,
Mid-continent Research for Education and Learning

an imprint of Capstone Press
Mankato, Minnesota

A+ Books are published by Capstone Press
151 Good Counsel Drive, P.O. Box 669, Mankato, Minnesota 56002
http://www.capstone-press.com

1 2 3 4 5 6 07 06 05 04 03 02

*Library of Congress Cataloging-in-Publication Data*
Schuette, Sarah L., 1976–
     Red / by Sarah L. Schuette.
     p.cm.—(Colors)
     Summary: Text and photographs describe common things that are red, including apples, red licorice,
and stop signs.
     Includes bibliographical references and index.
     ISBN 0-7368-1471-X (hardcover)
     1. Red—Juvenile literature. [1. Red.] I. Title.
QC495.5 .S367 2003
535.6—dc21                                                                                          2002000705

**Created by the A+ Team**
**Sarah L. Schuette, editor; Heather Kindseth, designer; Gary Sundermeyer, photographer;**
     **Nancy White, photo stylist**

*A+ Books thanks Michael Dahl for editorial assistance.*

**Note to Parents, Teachers, and Librarians**

The Colors series uses full-color photographs and a nonfiction format to introduce children to the world
of color. *Red* is designed to be read aloud to a pre-reader or to be read independently by an early reader.
Photographs and activities help early readers and listeners understand the text and concepts discussed.
The book encourages further learning by including the following sections: Table of Contents, Words to
Know, Read More, Internet Sites, and Index. Early readers may need assistance using these features.

# Table of Contents

Red has petals.
Red has thorns.

5

Fire trucks move fast to get to fires quickly. Many fire trucks are red so that people can see them racing down the street.

Red has flashing lights and horns.

Red is shiny.
Red is slick.

Cherries are sweet and juicy. Most cherries have a pit inside. Some people put cherries on top of ice cream sundaes.

Red strawberries always have green goosebumps. Strawberries are the only fruit with seeds on the outside.

Red is small and fun to pick.

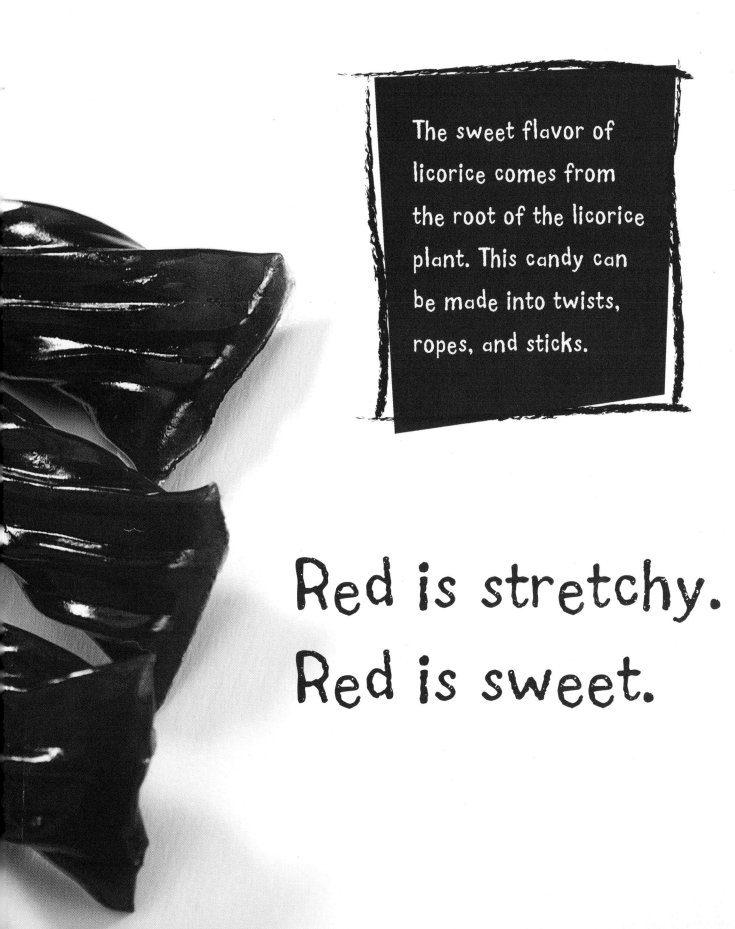

The sweet flavor of licorice comes from the root of the licorice plant. This candy can be made into twists, ropes, and sticks.

Red is stretchy.
Red is sweet.

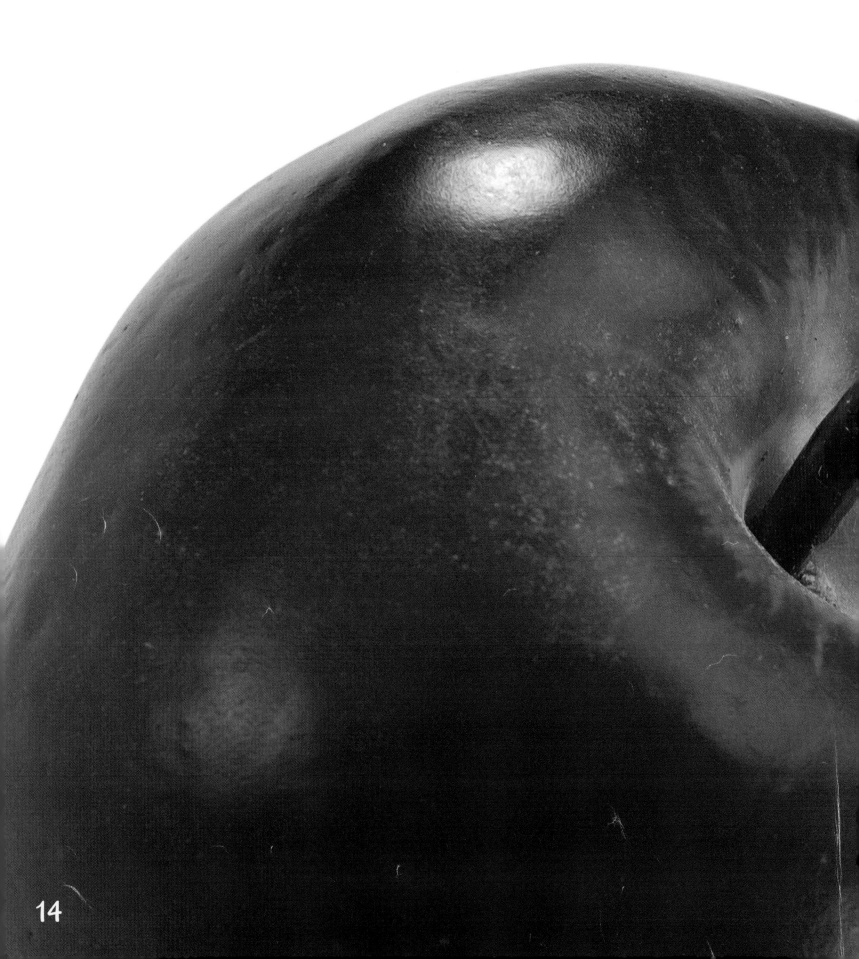

14

# Red is round and good to eat.

You can pick and eat a ripe red apple right from an apple tree. Apples can be baked in pies or cooked to make applesauce.

# Red splashes in the rain.

Red rubber boots keep your feet dry in the rain. Rubber is used to make boots and raincoats.

# Red twists around a cane.

Candy makers made the first candy canes by hand. They had to twist and bend each cane.

20

# Red makes cars slow down and stop.

Stop signs are always red with white letters. Red makes people think of danger.

22

# Red is curly
# on the top.

Red hair can be curly,
wavy, or straight. Other
names for red are ruby
and rose.

24

Cardinals have a crest of red feathers on top of their head. The crest looks like a hat.

# Red flies high and red sings.

Red can be
many things!

# Mixing Red

Artists use a color wheel to know how to mix colors. Red, blue, and yellow are primary colors. They mix together to make secondary colors. Purple, orange, and green are the secondary colors they make. You can use red to make orange and purple.

## You will need

red, yellow, and blue frosting
2 small plates
2 spoons
cupcakes

color wheel

**1** Put a small amount of red frosting onto each plate. Add the same amount of yellow frosting to one plate. Mix the two colors together with the tip of a spoon. What color do you see?

**2** Next, add the same amount of blue frosting to the second plate and mix the two colors together. What color do you see?

**3** Use the spoons to spread the orange and purple frosting on top of the cupcakes. Eat the cupcakes for a snack.

# Words to Know

feather—one of the light, fluffy parts that cover a bird's body; some birds have red feathers.

fruit—the fleshy, juicy part of a plant that people eat; apples, cherries, and strawberries are red fruits.

petal—one of the colored outer parts of a flower; red roses have soft and thin petals.

pit—the hard seed in the middle of some fruits, such as cherries

root—the part of a plant or tree that grows underground; roots bring water and food from the soil to the stem of a plant or to the trunk of a tree.

rubber—a material made from the sap of the rubber tree; sap flows through the trunk of the tree.

seed—the part of a flowering plant that can grow into a new plant; apple trees can grow from apple seeds.

# Read More

Harshman, Marc, and Cheryl Ryan. *Red Are the Apples.* San Diego: Gulliver Books, 2001.

Thong, Roseanne. *Red Is a Dragon: A Book of Colors.* San Francisco: Chronicle Books, 2001.

Whitehouse, Patricia. *Red Foods.* Colors We Eat. Chicago: Heinemann Library, 2002.

# Internet Sites

I Love Colors—Red
http://www.enchantedlearning.com/colors/red.shtml

Red PaintBear
http://www.thelittleartist.com/Red.html

Red! Red! Red!
http://www.umkc.edu/imc/red.htm

# Index